2/05

# GEOGRAPHY OF THE WORLD
## THE MYSTERIOUS
# AMAZON

*By Charnan Simon*

THE CHILD'S WORLD®
CHANHASSEN, MINNESOTA

**The Child's World**

Published in the United States of America by The Child's World®
PO Box 326, Chanhassen, MN 55317-0326
800-599-READ
www.childsworld.com

Content Adviser:
Jordan Clayton,
Geography Doctoral
Candidate, University
of Colorado, Boulder,
Colorado

Photo Credits: Cover/frontispiece: Layne Kennedy/Corbis.
Interior: Animals Animals/Earth Scenes: 8 (Fabio Colombini Medeiros), 14 (Michael Fogden); Miguel Rio Branco/Magnum Photos: 19, 26; Corbis: 4 (Yann Arthus-Bertrand), 15 (Jeffrey L. Rotman); OSF/Animals Animals/Earth Scenes: 12 (M. Fogden), 25 (R. Cousins); Wolfgang Kaehler/Corbis: 6, 9; Magnum Photos: 5 (Stuart Franklin), 13 (Bruno Barbey), 23 (Alex Webb); Nigel J. H. Smith/Animals Animals/Earth Scenes: 16, 18, 21.

The Child's World®: Mary Berendes, Publishing Director

Editorial Directions, Inc.: E. Russell Primm, Editorial Director; Melissa McDaniel, Line Editor; Katie Marsico, Associate Editor; Judi Shiffer, Associate Editor and Library Media Specialist; Matthew Messbarger, Editorial Assistant; Susan Hindman, Copy Editor; Sarah E. De Capua and Lucia Raatma, Proofreaders; Marsha Bonnoit, Peter Garnham, Terry Johnson, Olivia Nellums, Chris Simms, Katherine Trickle, and Stephen Carl Wender, Fact Checkers; Tim Griffin/IndexServ, Indexer; Cian Loughlin O'Day, Photo Researcher; Linda S. Koutris, Photo Selector; XNR Productions, Inc., Cartographer

The Design Lab: Kathleen Petelinsek, Design and Page Production

**Library of Congress Cataloging-in-Publication Data**
Simon, Charnan.
  The mysterious Amazon / by Charnan Simon.
    p. cm. — (Geography of the world)
  Includes index.
  ISBN 1-59296-336-6 (library bound : alk. paper) 1. Amazon River—Juvenile literature. 2. Amazon River Valley—Juvenile literature. I. Title. II. Geography of the world series.
  F2546.S663 2005
  918.1'1—dc22                                      2004003717

# Table of Contents

# CHAPTER ONE

# THE COURSE OF THE RIVER

The Amazon River is the biggest river in the world. It isn't the longest—the Nile River in Africa holds that record. But of all the rivers in the world, the Amazon is the widest and carries the most water. One-fifth of all the river water on earth flows through the Amazon.

**THE AMAZING AMAZON**
The Amazon carries 11 times more water than the Mississippi River. In fact, it holds more water than the next eight largest rivers in the world combined. The water pouring out of the Amazon could fill a million bathtubs in less than a minute!

*The Amazon is the longest river in South America. More than 200 of its tributaries flow through Brazil (shown here).*

The Amazon River begins as a tiny, icy stream high in the Andes Mountains of Peru, in South America. As it tumbles down the mountains, it is joined by countless other streams and rivers called **tributaries.** As many as 15,000 tributaries flow into the Amazon River system. The

*The scenic Negro River stretches 1,400 miles (2,250 km) and is the largest of all the Amazon's tributaries.*

largest of these—the Negro, Madeira, Tapajós, and Xingu—are major rivers in their own right.

After the Amazon pours down from the Andes, it flows eastward through an enormous river **basin.** This basin covers almost half of South America. It includes much of Brazil and parts of Peru, Bolivia, Venezuela, Colombia, Ecuador, Guyana, Suriname, and French Guiana. The Amazon basin is almost as big as the whole United States.

*The Amazon rain forest covers more than 2.3 million square miles*
*(6 sq km) and is considered one of the biggest rain forests on earth.*

For most of its course, the Amazon flows through dense tropical

**rain forest.** With its thousands of tributaries, the Amazon is more

like a vast sea of rivers than a single flowing stream. Its main channel

ranges from about 2 miles (3 kilometers) wide in the dry season to as

much as 40 miles (64 km) wide during the rainy season. And what a

rainy season it is! For several months every year, rain pours steadily for

six or seven hours a day. The river overflows its banks and floods the forest for miles around. Plants, animals, and people have adapted to

this flooding. Spiders and ground insects seek shelter high in the trees.

Flooded meadows provide safe "nurseries" where young fish find plen-

ty of food. People build their houses on stilts and make floating rafts

for their pigs and cows. Fish swim among the branches looking for

fruit, too! When they swim downstream,

the spread undigested seeds for miles

around. The fish need fruit from flooded

trees to survive. The trees need fish to

spread their seeds.

When the rainy season ends, the

sun comes out and dries up the flood-

**SEASONS OF THE AMAZON**
**It is always warm in the Amazon rain forest. There isn't a cold season and a warm season, as in most of the United States. Instead, there is a high-water season and a low-water season. During the high-water season, the river rises as much as 30 feet (9 meters).**

waters. Birds eat worms and small fish in the shallow ponds and rich

mud left behind. People plant fast-growing crops such as watermelons,

bans, rice, and manioc. Rain forest plant grow lush and green.

Finally, after flowing some 4,000 miles (6,437 km), the Amazon

empties into the Atlantic Ocean. Here, in the delta—the flat land at the river's mouth—the Amazon drops much of the **sediment** it has picked up on its journey. This sediment creates a maze of islands that separates the Amazon into many channels. During the high-water season, the mouth of the Amazon can stretch for nearly 300 miles (483 km). The river pours a stream of freshwater into the ocean that continues flowing for more than 150 miles (383 km)!

*The Amazon's high-water season lasts from December until May.*
*During this season, low-lying land often floods.*

# CHAPTER TWO

# PLANTS AND ANIMALS

No other place on earth supports as much plant and animal life as the Amazon River basin. It's hard to imagine just how many creatures call the Amazon home.

Scientists think that up to one-third of all the plants on earth live in the Amazon. There may be as many as 80,000 **species** of trees and 55,000 species of flowering plants. Half of these flowering plants are found nowhere else on earth. A single acre of Amazon rain forest can support 3,000 different plant species.

Animal life in the Amazon is just as amazing. Ten percent of earth's animals live in the Amazon basin. More species

*Colorful bromeliads (broh-MEE-lee-ads) grow in the Amazon rain forest. There are about 2500 different varieties of this tropical plant, and some can reach a height of 20 feet (6 m)!*

of fish live in the Amazon than in the entire Atlantic Ocean. So far, scientists have identified 1,700 of these species—but there may be as many as 4,000. The Amazon is home to 500 species of catfish alone!

One-fifth of the world's birds live in the Amazon rain forest. Noisy flocks of parrots and toucans fly through the greenery. Tiny hummingbirds dart from flower to flower, and huge harpy eagles watch from the treetops.

More than 200 different kinds of mammals call the Amazon home--plus at least 50 kinds of bats! The world's smallest monkey lives there: the 6-inch, 6-ounce (15-cm, 170-gram) pygmy marmoset. One of the world's slowest animals can be found there, too. The two-toed sloth spends its life hanging upside down from a branch, sleeping most of the day. It moves from one branch to the next very slowly and only goes down to the ground about once a week.

*A map of the Amazon River*

The Amazon teems with lizards, frogs, snakes, turtles, and caimans (a member of the crocodilian family), especially during high-water season. As for insects—well, nobody knows exactly how many insects

*The little barred leaf frog has suction pads on its toes that help it to cling to smooth plant matter.*

and spiders live in the rain forest. Some experts say there are 15,000 different kinds— others say there could be 60 million varieties!

From above, the Amazon rain forest looks like a solid sea of green. But it is really made up of several different layers. Each layer is home to its own plants and animals.

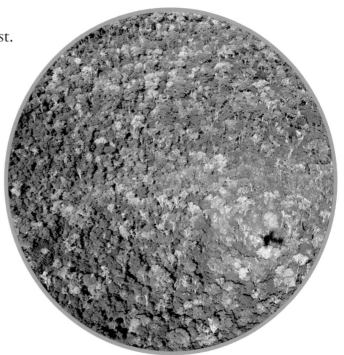

*A view from the air reveals the emerald canopy of the Brazilian rain forest. The canopy is home to a wide range of animals, including birds, butterflies, monkeys, and bats.*

The canopy is the forest's ceiling. Most trees in the rain forest grow to about the same height—more than 100 feet (30 m). Their branches spread to form a solid layer, or canopy, over the rest of the forest. Every now and then, an especially tall tree, called an emergent, stands high above the rest. The best leaves and fruits for eating are found in the canopy, so that's where the most birds and animals are found, too.

*Plants that grow on the rain forest floor often have larger leaves that help them to absorb what little sunlight makes its way through the canopy.*

Below the canopy is the understory. The understory is made up of bushes, shrubs, vines, and smaller trees. The understory is a dark place, which animals pass through to reach the canopy or the forest floor.

Hardly any sunlight reaches the rain forest floor. Worms, insects, and **fungi** feed on fallen fruits and leaves. Small animals such as anteaters and capybaras roam through this area. Larger animals such as deer and jaguars feed near clearings and small streams.

# CHAPTER THREE

# THE AMAZON, PAST AND PRESENT

The Amazon River basin is one of the most **sparsely** populated places in the world. The dense jungle makes it practically impossible to travel by land, and snakes and mosquitoes make life difficult for people who do.

*A resident of the rain forest carefully crosses a bridge made of tree branches and logs. Just as you have to watch for traffic and avoid strangers, inhabitants of the rain forest need to be on the lookout for dangerous animals and changes in landscape.*

*Marajó Island is the world's largest river island. It measures 183 miles (295 km) long and 124 miles (200 km) wide.*

Still, historians think that people have lived along the Amazon in Brazil, Colombia, and Peru for 11,000 years. Scientists have found remains of beautifully decorated pottery on Marajó Island, near the mouth of the Amazon. They think as many as 100,000 people may have lived on or near Marajó a thousand years ago.

The earliest people in the region probably didn't live right on the banks of the river. Floods were too dangerous. But the people still depended on the river for transportation and food. In fact, fishing was so important to Amazonian life that some early people called them-selves *Wai Mahi*—"fish people."

Spanish and Portuguese explorers first reached South America in the 1490s. By 1500, Portugal had claimed the land that is now Brazil. At first, Europeans were looking for gold in the Amazon River basin. Later, they sought valuable products such as mahogany wood, turtle eggs, and spices such as cloves and cinnamon. They grew sugar and tobacco on huge farms. The Europeans used Indians as slaves to do the hard work for them. By 1700, about 90 percent of these Indians had been killed by massacres, European diseases, and the abuses of slavery.

In the mid-1800s, there was a rubber boom in the Amazon. The world needed rubber for automobile tires and other products. The raw material to

## PINZÓN'S AMAZING DISCOVERY

In January 1500, Spanish explorer Vicente Yáñez Pinzón was sailing off the east coast of South America. He was so far out to sea—more than 100 miles (161 km)—that he couldn't see the shore. Imagine his surprise when he noticed that the water splashing up against his ship was freshwater, not salty. Pinzón pointed his ship toward shore and sailed into what looked like a huge inland sea. He had discovered the Amazon River.

*Latex drains into a bucket attached to a rubber tree. Rubber trees continue to be among the most economically important trees in the Amazon.*

make this rubber—a white, sticky substance called latex—oozed out of the bark of certain rain forest trees. Once again, Europeans used the native people for the hard work of collecting this latex. Many more thousands of Indians died doing this work before the rubber boom ended in the early 1900s.

Today, mining, fishing, logging, and cattle ranching are important industries in the Amazon. Most people in the Amazon basin live in large cities. But some native people still live in small settlements along the river.

*Workers labor in a Brazilian gold mine. Unfortunately, gold mining in the Amazon has raised environmental concerns due to chemicals that are often released into nearby streams and rivers.*

# CHAPTER FOUR

# A USEFUL RIVER

As long as people have lived in the Amazon basin, the river has been an important highway. From dugout canoes to great ocean-going ships, people have always depended on the river to transport them and their goods from place to place.

Today, ships carry fuel, grain, tools, and other goods up the river to large cities such as Belém, Santarém, and Manaus. Smaller ships sail all the way to the foothills of the Andes. After they unload, they fill up with fish, timber, and other products that are sent to the rest of the world.

Logging and mining are major industries along the Amazon. Loggers cut down trees deep in the rain forest. Then they float the logs downriver. The logs are sawed into lumber and shipped to the rest of the world.

## THE WORLD'S MEDICINE CABINET

Many Amazon rain forest plants are used as medicines. Scientists estimate that one-fourth of all the medicines currently used originally came from rain forests around the world. But scientists are worried. They haven't had time to study anywhere near all the plants in the Amazon. Yet huge areas of the rain forest are being chopped down every day. What if important medicines are disappearing with the trees?

*Within recent years, certain restrictions have been placed on logging in order to prevent further destruction of the rain forest.*

**HALF A GROCERY STORE**
Coffee, cinnamon, cloves, Brazil nuts, cashew nuts, peanuts, potatoes, rice, tea, lemons, oranges, pineapples, grapefruit, peanuts, sugar, and cocoa are just a few of the foods that come from the Amazon rain forest.

The region is also rich in gold and iron ores. Underground are vast stores of oil.

Unfortunately, all of this activity has not been good for the Amazon rain forest. Logging and mining damage the environment and cause pollution. Clearing away trees destroys the habitats of plants and animals. It also allows more soil to wash away into the river. This has led to many species of plants and animals becoming endangered. If the Amazon is to remain healthy, people must find new and better ways to live and work along the river.

# CHAPTER FIVE

# PEOPLE ALONG THE RIVER

Native Indians were the first people to live in the Amazon River basin. European settlers—mainly from Spain and Portugal—began arriving in the 1500s. And, between about 1600 and the late 1800s, more than 3 million African men, women, and children were brought to the Amazon as slaves. Today, many of the people who live along the Amazon are of mixed heritage—part Indian, part European, and part African.

Most of these people live in large cities such as Iquitos and Pucallpa in Peru, and Manaus, Belém, and Santarém in Brazil. But more and more people are moving to new settlements being carved out of the rain forest. These settlers chop down trees to build their homes. They burn other trees to make fields for growing crops or raising cattle. Bulldozers clear roads deep into the heart of the rain forest. The settlers need homes to live in and food to eat. But many people are worried about how fast the rain forest is being destroyed.

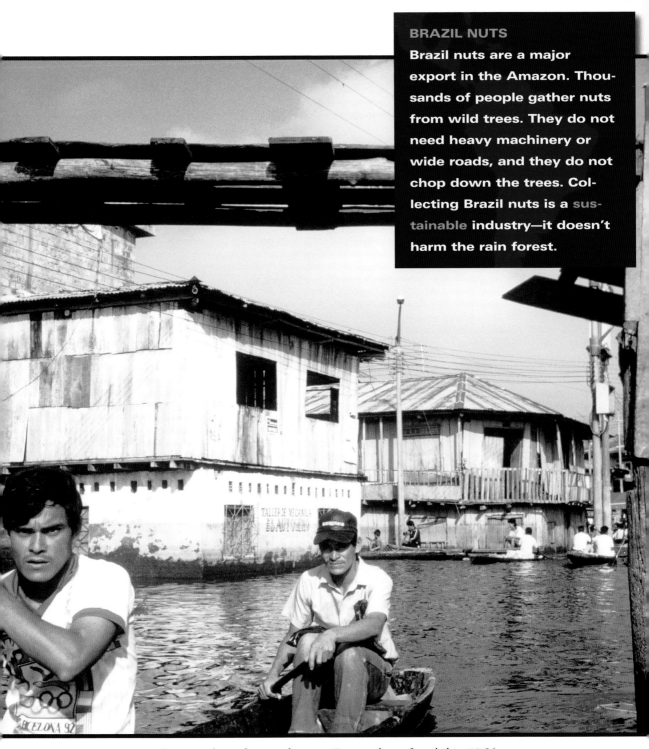

*Iquitos is located in northeastern Peru and was founded in 1864.*
*It is currently home to more than 300,000 residents.*

Some people continue to live in harmony with the river, much as their ancestors have for hundreds of years. They live in small clearings and build simple houses on stilts to keep them safe during high-water season. They plant quick-growing crops such as watermelons, bananas, and manioc, which have time to ripen during low-water season. They fish and hunt in traditional ways. They gather just enough rain forest fruits and medicinal plants to stay healthy. And every few years, they move to a new location, allowing the rain forest to grow back.

Rubber tappers also live in harmony with the rain forest. Although the rubber boom of the 19th century has ended, latex is still an important export in the Amazon basin. Rubber trees are among the most common trees in the rain forest. Taking latex does not harm the trees. Today, more than 500,000 rubber tappers collect latex from rubber trees, in much the same way as New England farmers tap maple trees for sap to make syrup.

MANIOC

Manioc is a root vegetable that is popular throughout the Amazon. You may have eaten manioc in tapioca pudding. People in the Amazon grind some kinds of manioc into flour to make bread, pancakes, and porridge. They boil or mash other kinds of manioc the way we cook potatoes.

# CHAPTER SIX

# LOOKING TO THE FUTURE

The Amazon River basin has changed more in the past 40 years than in the previous 400 years. It is estimated that every minute of every day, a piece of the rain forest the size of 14 football fields disappears.

This loss of the rain forest affects the whole planet. The Amazon rain forest has sometimes been called "the lungs of the world." Its trees and plants are constantly taking a gas called carbon dioxide from the air and turning it into oxygen that people and animals breathe. Fewer trees means less oxygen. And burning down the forest releases even more carbon dioxide into the air. Some scientists fear this is harming earth.

*If rainforests such as this one continue to be cleared, scientists will never have an opportunity to learn about new species of plants and animals that have yet to be discovered.*

## A WET DESERT

Half the rainfall in the Amazon basin comes from—trees! Here's how: Rain falls to the forest floor, where trees take it in through their roots. The trees then slowly release water back into the air during photosynthesis. The evaporated water is called water vapor. This water vapor forms local rain clouds. Rain falls, and the whole cycle starts again. The rain forest is a wet place. But without trees to help provide rainfall, it would be more like a desert.

*Animals ranging from the tiniest tree frog to the most fearsome jaguar would all be in trouble if the Amazon became a desert wasteland.*

Once a large section of rain forest has been chopped down or burned, it is hard for it to grow back. Without trees to make shade, the land is baked hard by the hot sun during low-water season. Without plant roots to hold rainwater and soil, floods wash away the land during high-water season.

Without shelter and food, animals and insects move away or die. The rain forest becomes a desert wasteland.

The river, too, has become polluted. Mining companies use poisonous chemicals to refine gold and iron. These chemicals often end up in the Amazon and its tributaries. They kill fish and plants and threaten the entire natural world.

The countries in the Amazon River basin have many poor citizens. These people want to use the land, water, and mineral resources of the rain forest to help their families live better lives. Who can blame them? The Amazon basin is so huge that it might seem as if the natural resources will never run out.

But without careful planning, this is exactly what will happen. Today, governments and environmental groups are working together. They are trying to find ways to balance the needs of the rain forest with the needs of people. If they succeed, the Amazon River basin will remain one of our planet's greatest treasures for many years to come.

## DAMS—GOOD OR BAD?

You like having electricity to light your house and provide power for your computer, don't you? People in the Amazon basin like electricity in their homes, too. They have built dams on their rivers to produce this electricity. Using water to create electricity is cleaner than burning coal and oil. But dams can also drown river valleys and change the flooding patterns in the rain forest. Sometimes, what helps people hurts the natural world.

# Glossary

**basin (BAY-suhn)** A river basin is the low-lying land that is drained by a river and its tributaries. After the Amazon pours down from the Andes, it flows eastward through an enormous river basin.

**fungi (FUHN-jye)** Fungi are tiny organisms that break down and feed on other, usually dead, organisms. Fungi feed on fallen fruits and leaves in the Amazon rain forest.

**habitats (HAB-uh-tats)** Habitats are places where certain kinds of plants or animals naturally live. The Amazon river basin provides an astonishing variety of habitats.

**photosynthesis (foh-toh-SIN-thuh-siss)** A chemical process by which green plants make their food. Plants use energy from the sun to turn water and carbon dioxide into food, and they give off oxygen as a by-product.

**rain forest (RAIN FOR-ust)** A rain forest is a region that receives a lot of rain and usually has a very wide variety of plant and animal life. For most of its course, the Amazon River runs through a rain forest.

**sediment (SED-uh-muhnt)** Sediment is small pieces of dirt and rock that are carried along by a river and then sink to the river bottom. When the Amazon flood waters recede, rich sediments are left behind.

**sparsely (SPARSS-lee)** Sparsely describes how an area is populated. Not many people live in sparsely populated areas.

**species (SPEE-sheez)** A species is a particular kind of plant or animal. As many as 80,000 species of trees and 55,000 species of flowering plants live along the Amazon River.

**sustainable (suh-STAYN-uh-buhl)** An industry is sustainable if it does not harm the environment or use up the resources that it depends on. Collecting Brazil nuts is a sustainable activity.

**tributaries (TRIB-yuh-ter-eez)** Tributaries are smaller streams or rivers that flow into a larger river. The Amazon's largest tributaries are the Negro, the Madeira, the Tapajos, and the Xingu rivers.

# An Amazon River Almanac

**Names:** None

**Extent**
    Length: 4,000 miles (6,437 km)—
        world's second longest river
    Width: 2 to 40 miles (3.2 to 64.4 km)
    Depth: 50 to 160 feet (15.2 to 48.8 m)

**Continent:** South America

**Countries:** Bolivia, Brazil, Colombia, Ecuador, French Guiana, Guyana, Peru, Suriname, and Venezuela

**Major tributaries:** Branco, Jari, Juruá, Madeira, Negro, Purus, Tapajós, Trombetas, and Xingu

**Major cities:** Belém, Manaus, Óbidos, Santarém (Brazil); Iquitos, Pucallpa (Peru)

**Major languages:** Dutch, English, French, Portuguese, Quechua, and Spanish

**Parks and preserves:** Jau National Park (Brazil); Cuyabeno Reserve, Limoncocha Biological Reserve, Upper Napo Preserve, Yasuní National Park (Ecuador); Manú National Park, Pacaya-Samiria National Reserve (Peru)

**Natural resources:** Gold, iron ore, lumber, oil, and rubber

**Native birds:** 1,750 species, including harpy eagles, hummingbirds, parrots, and toucans

**Native fish:** At least 1,700 species, including 500 species of catfish

**Native mammals:** Bats, capybaras, jaguars, monkeys, and toe-toed sloths

**Native reptiles:** Caimans, lizards, and snakes

**Native plants:** 55,000 species of flowering plants, including bromeliads, ferns, mosses, orchids, vines; 80,000 species of trees

**Major products:** Animal skins, Brazil nuts, cashew nuts, cocoa, coffee, fruit, live birds and fish for pet shops, lumber, peanuts, plants for medicines, rice, rubber, spices, sugar, and tea

# The Amazon River in the News

| | |
|---|---|
| **A.D. 1000** | It is believed that as many as 100,000 people may have lived on or near Marajó Island, which is located close to the mouth of the Amazon. Archaeologists think that people have probably lived along the Amazon in Brazil, Colombia, and Peru for 11,000 years. |
| **1500** | The Portuguese claim Brazil as a colony, resulting in trade between Europeans and native Brazilians. While sailing off the east coast of South America in January, Spanish explorer Vicente Yáñez Pinzón discovers the Amazon River. |
| **1541–1542** | Spanish soldier Francisco de Orellana sails downstream on the Amazon and travels from the Peruvian Andes to the Atlantic Ocean. |
| **1600–late 1800s** | More than 3 million Africans are brought to the Amazon as slaves. |
| **1637–1638** | Spanish explorer Pedro Teixeira sails upstream on the Amazon and travels from the Andes to Quito, Ecuador. |
| **1700** | Because of their contact with Europeans, 90 percent of the native peoples who once lived along the Amazon are dead by this time. They were wiped out by slavery, massacres, and diseases such as smallpox and measles. |
| **1799–1805** | Prussian scientist and explorer Baron Alexander von Humboldt journeys through South America and Central America. At this time, he also maps much of the area and shows that the Amazon and Orinoco rivers are connected. |
| **mid-1800s** | A rubber boom occurs, and the demand for latex (found in the bark of certain Amazonian rain forest trees) rises. |
| **1848–1859** | English scientist H. W. Bates visits the Amazon region and takes notes about the people and animals he observes. |
| **1863** | W. H. Bates publishes *The Naturalist on the River Amazons*. This book includes observations Bates made while living along the Amazon. |
| **1913–1914** | Former U.S. president Theodore Roosevelt and Brazilian colonel Cândido Rondon explore the Madeira River, which is a tributary of the Amazon. |
| **1992** | The United Nations Conference on Environment and Development (also called the Earth Summit) is held in Rio de Janeiro, Brazil. At this meeting, efforts are made to protect the environment and to limit the clearing of tropical rain forests. |

# How to Learn More about the Amazon River

## At the Library

Cherry, Lynn. *The Great Kapok Tree.* San Diego: Harcourt Brace and Company, 1990.

Furnweger, Karen. *Amazon Rising: Seasons of the River.* Chicago: Shedd Aquarium, 2000.

Goodman, Susan E. *Bats, Bugs, and Biodiversity: Adventures in the Amazonian Rain Forest.*
New York: Atheneum, 1995.

Murray, Peter. *The Amazon.* Chanhassen, Minn.: The Child's World, 1994.

Nesbitt, Kris. *My Amazon River Day.* Chicago: Shedd Aquarium, 2000.

Parker, Edward. *The Amazon.* Milwaukee: World Almanac Library, 2003.

## On the Web

VISIT OUR HOME PAGE FOR LOTS OF LINKS ABOUT THE AMAZON RIVER:
*http://www.childsworld.com/links.html*

Note to Parents, Teachers, and Librarians: We routinely verify our Web links to make sure
they are safe, active sites—so encourage your readers to check them out!

## Places to Visit or Contact

EMBASSY OF BRAZIL
3006 Massachusetts Avenue NW
Washington, DC 20008-3634

EMBASSY OF ECUADOR
2535 15th Street NW
Washington, DC 20009

EMBASSY OF PERU
1700 Massachusetts Avenue NW
Washington, DC 20036

# Index

## About the Author

**Charnan Simon** has a BA in English literature from Carleton College and an MA in English literature from the University of Chicago. She has been an editor at both *Cricket* and *Click* magazines and has written more than 50 books for young readers. Ms. Simon lives in Madison, Wisconsin, with her husband Tom, their daughters, Ariel and Hana, Sam the dog, and Lily and Luna the cats.